A GREEN BOUGH

A Green Bough

Poems for Renewal

NANCY CORSON CARTER

RESOURCE *Publications* • Eugene, Oregon

A GREEN BOUGH
Poems for Renewal

Resource Publications
An Imprint of Wipf and Stock Publishers
199 W. 8th Ave., Suite 3
Eugene, OR 97401

www.wipfandstock.com

PAPERBACK ISBN: 978-1-5326-9144-7
HARDCOVER ISBN: 978-1-5326-9145-4
EBOOK ISBN: 978-1-5326-9146-1

Manufactured in the U.S.A.   AUGUST 27, 2019

for Howard, Rebecca, and Gustavo

and for all who love and care for the Earth

If I keep a green bough in my heart, the singing bird will come.

—old Chinese saying

Contents

III   Unexpected Allies | 59

Preface

A central theme of my work is nurturing our human interconnections with the entire world of nature, both its physical and spiritual aspects. A Pennsylvania child fortunate to have parents and grandparents who farmed and gardened, I understood myself as part of a great community of life. My first poem, written in second grade, celebrated farmers as well as rain, flowers, and birds in springtime.

In graduate school I wrote my M.A. thesis on Henry David Thoreau. Later, at a Presbyterian women's retreat on the Psalms, I felt called to work for eco-justice; this is now a central mission for me. In that same decade, the 1980s, I launched a course at Eckerd College that expressed the heart of my concerns: "Literature and Ecology: Writings About the Earth Household." Over the years, we studied works by such fine writers as Terry Tempest Williams, Aldo Leopold, John Muir, Gary Snyder, Leslie Marmon Silko, Thomas Berry, Black Elk, Rachel Carson, Annie Dillard, and Barry Lopez. I continue to be inspired by such poets as Denise Levertov, Mary Oliver, W.S. Merwin, Wendell Berry, and William Stafford.

Increasingly, however, our Earth household is challenged by living on a severely threatened planet. For this book I have chosen a title and epigraph that express my hope that we humans will respond with committed urgency to heal and to protect Earth's health and beauty.

I seek to learn from the wisdom of many traditions that honor the holy heart of the world, its deep spirit. From my own tradition, I explore the tensions of the central Christian mystery: the inevitability of suffering and loss, but also the power of redeeming grace. I offer these poems—that range in moods from praise and play to lament and hope—as a green bough for all who cherish the Tree of Life.

Acknowledgments

Thanks for so many who have generously given support and encouragement in my writing life, especially my husband, Howard Carter, whose excellent editing and steadfast companionship I cherish.

My grateful acknowledgment of the following publications in which some of the poems in this collection first appeared, some in slightly different form:

Anima Poetry: "Succession of the Gypsy King"

Bellowing Ark: "Love Has No Common Sense," "Unexpected Festivity," "Kinglet," "Optics—a Love Poem" retitled as "Optics Matter: A Love Poem"; "Mountain Views: Missoula, Montana" retitled as "A Sojourner's Views"

Christianity and Literature: "Opening and Closing Doors: Lessons for Novices"

CommonSense 2, online journal: "Designer Earth: A Do-It-Yourself Vision"

Cotyledon: two of the "Mountain Views: Missoula, Montana" retitled as "A Sojourner's Views"

IMPROV: Anthology of Grassroots Poets: "Call and Response"

The Lutheran Digest: "Rx for Peace"

Modern Haiku: "snow clouds thicken"

Pilgrimage: "The Deer Bid Good-bye," "A Rat Occasions Reluctant Prayer"

St. Petersburg Evening Independent: "The Jacaranda Fantasy"

Society for Values in Higher Education Newsletter: "Reading Downstream"

Survivors' Box, ed. Margaret R. Rigg: "Tintagel"

Tiferet: "Among Dry Rocks, Water"

Unbound: An Interactive Journal of Christian Social Justice: "Sanctuary of the Mountain Sunrise," "Madonna and Child Sheltering Supplicants Under Her Cloak," "Avocado Picking on the Sabbath"

I

The Green World

Waiting for Angels

*The secret of waiting is the faith that the seed
has been planted, that something has begun.*

—Henri Nouwen

Too old to have another child,
I sometimes think of Sarah.
If angels visit to proclaim
astonishing news,
I promise not to laugh.

At 4:30 a.m. we scan for
November Leonid showers.
None sighted, but the sky's
belly swells with promise.

In early light I find
a praying mantis egg case
on the garden fence.

We dig in daffodil bulbs
with vole-deterrent gravel,
then cover, tamp, and water,
just before first frost.

The deer change coats;
the pines brace and hum.

I don't see angels
though I sometimes hear wings;
like the daytime stars,
I know they are there.

Washing My Car in the Rain
Under the Fig Tree

The rain's pattering feels
cool and tender;
it doesn't matter that I get wet.

With T-shirt rag I rub
that tricky area around
the Ford's roof rack.

Careful not to throw my back out
or slice fingers on metal edges,
I scrub slowly, rinsing

with rain barrel stores
now overflowing
from daily showers.

A lush abundance, like
Hildegard's "greening
world" embraces all.

I breathe our fig's fragrance,
hope brushing branches
won't convey chiggers.

Within leafy depths
I spy coming harvest:
tiny gourd-shaped fruits

of ripening sweetness
I'll race the ants
to claim.

*Hildegard "of Bingen," Germany,
founded an abbey (1147 CE) and often
preached on God's love for all creation.*

Avocado Picking on the Sabbath

for Bill Wilbur

How lucky to have a friend
who, after church, invited us
to glean avocados
wind-fallen from his trees.

With childish glee,
we filled grocery bags
with green, glossy fruit
and imagined grand feasting.

Cooling shadows
arched over us
as we bent in noon heat
to the sumptuous task.

But then our sun-laced idyll
took an unexpected turn:
the shadows began to
multiply and move.

Great silhouettes
overhead swashed
the blue satin sky
with scimitar wings—

Magnificent Frigatebirds!
Rare Swallow-tailed Kites!
Their regal black and white
bodies created a vortex

of stroboscopic sunlight
hypnotically glittering.
As we spiraled upward
to alleluias of angels,

we glimpsed grand visions
of all things renewed
and crowds brunching gaily
on divine guacamole.

The Jacaranda Fantasy

In springtime I say to every guest
"You mustn't go until the jacaranda blooms—
you will never forget its beauty;
it is the tree of heaven."

And so they wait, and so they are rewarded
when frilled blue-purple petals
shower from the sky.
"See? What did I tell you?"

Up in the tree they are
        sipping spicy nectar,
        singing with birds,
        conversing with clouds.

They're blue-purple euphoric
as I yearn to be soon,
but first all my dear ones
must be summoned and launched.

When all are assembled,
I float up to join them
in a jacaranda hammock.

We debate the color's name:
        periwinkle, lilac, mist,
        heather, amethyst, cerulean . . .
None quite suffice,

So we begin to invent:
   third-eye-open purple,
   nightingales-in-moonlight orchid,
   shadow-under-your-earlobe-where-I-
    long-to-nibble mauve . . .

Tiring of that game, we shower petals
on all who walk below us;
they give us blue-purple smiles
and go their ways dancing.

Petal-steeped shadows remind us of
   Monet's twilight haystacks,
   Chagall's cobalt windows,
   lavender lines à la Sappho.

Bees hum appreciatively
from blossom chalices;
they return to their hives
to make blue-purple honey.

Silk moths gorge on petals,
spin blue-purple cocoons;
we gather and weave them
into heavenly robes—

We'll wear these on feast days
of our patroness-friend,
the deliciously inimitable
St. Jacaranda.

Zacchaeus

"Zacchaeus, hurry and come down;
for I must stay at your house today."

—Luke 19:5b

From that dusty
sycamore he
called me down
to lift me up.

He cast out
my timid silence,
my hidden
hoarded shame.

He named my fear
of being seen for
what I was: a little man
of little meaning.

Perched precariously
on a breaking branch,
I took his hand,
came safely home.

Now I Zacchaeus
urge *you* to hasten:
be in your house his
host and guest today.

In him our meanest
wealth's transformed;
His love fills every tree
with unexpected harvest.

Platonic Tulips

for B.Z., who almost brought me
tulips from Holland

"They were your color—
glorious red-orange—
but illegal to import.
Sorry, but I gave them
to someone else."

Too late for apology.
I envision them seizing
faint morning light,
wringing it into gaudy sound;
they blow a mean Dutch jazz.

At noon, sootblack pistils
and gold-dusted stamens
spill watercolor hues
into wet paper air—
they seep through my smile.

For tea, they play royalty,
their ruby-topaz crowns
aloft on gold stems.
Leaves gloved in jade silk,
they gesture imperiously.

Meanwhile your intended
real tulips crumple and dry;
they wait on back stairs
for someone (that usurper!)
to replant them next spring.

But these imagined tulips
reveal in the moonlight
their quintessential form:
the silvery ghost
of a lover's bouquet.

Exotics at Large

Spotted Knapweed is high
on the Forest Service's Ten Most
Wanted List of Noxious Weeds;
it's a range wrecker.
One more pretty face
gone to bad seed—
even the elk can't stomach her.

Purple Loosestrife—
we knew right away
she didn't belong,
not among us proper folk—
a salacious color and
not choosy about being out,
anywhere, anytime, with anyone.

Dalmatian Toadflax
looks like a snapdragon
dressed in sunshiny yellows.
She loves romping
with fleet spotted dogs,
playing runaway fire truck
out on a call.

But that's just a con;
she's in league with mobsters
like cheatgrass, locoweed,
and hemp dogbane. Her seeds
spread like wildfire and last
a decade. The poor native
plants can't take her heat.

Petunias

That dusty-warm fragrance! It takes me back to Aunt Viola's and Uncle Clete's porch in summer evening shadows. Flowers spill from cement urns on the stairs, their petals velvety as coats of little bats. My sisters and I whoosh back and forth in their wide swing, enveloped by that comfortable smell. After being good children at supper, this free, easy moment is specially ours. Years later, I remember it as I walk the grounds of Seton Hill, a Daughters of Charity shrine. It's late October. The gardeners obviously favor petunias. One bed curves toward the basilica while another circles an "officially blessed" white marble statue of Louise de Marillac, the order's founder. A vivid retinue blooms at her feet: luminous pale blues mix with plain reds and pinks; royal purples partner scarlets with white star throats. I imagine well-cared-for lovelies who preen and flutter in the sunshine. Some are little girls twirling in soft ruffled dresses. Others flirt with parasols in nonchalant sashay. Some, wide-wimpled nuns, serve as chaperones. Despite a sweet aura of endless promenade, they're all subject to autumn's whims. The next day, a chilly one, I find them disheveled by blustery rain. Our quixotic Indian Summer is over and gone.

Olives, Silver and Gold

Silver olive leaves
glisten with snow—
manna to the eye,
gone before noon.
But it's a minor miracle
compared to this:

From *terres ingrates*
of Bouches-du-Rhône,
through gnarled trunks,
the sun-seared fruit—
virgin oil flows uphill,
pours out golden.

Unexpected Festivity

Musky perfume distracts me
on my morning walk,
lures me round a corner
to encounter milky-flowered
Sabal Palm, as fecund as
the many-breasted
Ephesian Diana.

I watch honey bees, moths,
bumblebees, and wasps in
green metallic jackets;
all sport dandys' leggings
sticky-sweet with
creamy pollen.

Humming and thrumming,
their Rabelaisian fervor
rises with an approving sun.
Bumptious rites of spring,
hot Carnevale,
send me dashing, dizzied,
into cooling shade.

I think of Breughel's
lusty peasants whirling,
of Renoir's couples
flirting by the Seine,
of Tom Jones's
bawdy banquet revels.

Can such an invitation
be refused: to yield
to buzzing eros,
swoon away into
the woozy wanton
arms of flowers?

Remains of a Beach Day

Every wave magnifies
the dazzling—
a net of diamonds
rises, falls, rises . . .

High tide marks
the shore's shoulder like
delicate tracery
of a lover's fingertips.

Broken shells whoosh and
chinkle, ebbing and flowing;
pelicans skim swells
in long languid rows.

From just the right angle
we can see needlefish;
stand still and ghost crabs
skittle from hiding.

Hurricane-shredded palms
rattle in salt wind;
swaths of shadows
sweep white sand.

I lost a gold earring here,
a tiny owl, Athena's familiar;
like a royal guard of memory
she keeps this day alive.

Among Dry Rocks, Water

for Bishop Baker Ochola
and all peacemakers

For months the stream bed
glimmered only where tiny
seeps threaded the stones.
Resurrection ferns
cringed on the banks;
the water's music stopped.

Yesterday I heard the story
of a Ugandan holy man.
In a world scorched
with violence, thirsting for joy,
he was christened "one of hope."

In slow straight words he told
of a daughter kidnapped,
raped, and shamed into suicide,
of a wife shattered by a landmine.

He spoke of love and courage
with irrefutable authority.
Shaking hands with him, I felt
a humbling power.

Now rain darkens the boulders;
mosses patch them in emerald—
signs, we hope, of drought ending.

Parched pools swell and chain,
restore the stream's flowing
until it spills over
the lip of the dam.

The Deer Bid Good-bye

Up at dawn,
       we race to meet
              the movers' deadline

Until we notice a presence
       that calms our frenzy:
              silhouettes

At cornfield's edge—
       three deer,
              a doe with fawns.

With steps soft as mist
       they nibble across
              the new-mown orchard.

For some precious moments
       packing up our homestead
              is only illusion:

We will stay forever,
       belonging as they do
              to fields, river, and mountains.

The doe waits, still,
       while her young play;
              their sweet wild grace

Arcs over us like a rainbow
       that fades, at last,
              back into the enveloping green.

II

Loss and Survival

Call and Response

A 2008 study at the Carmabi Foundation in Curaçao,
Dutch Antilles, found that baby corals swim toward
sound made by animals on a home reef.

An October moon swells,
luminous with life
soon reflected in
Earth's tropic waters:

her magic blue light
increases unique
protein genes that
click coral clocks ON.

Then a sperm-and-eggs orgy
of annual mass spawning
effervesces the seas
with tiny larvae;

true to long-ago coding
they swim for their lives
toward the choiring calls
of a mother reef's refuge.

What thwarts them most
is human-made noise like
pile-driving, shipping,
seismic testing, and drilling.

Their imperiled enchantment
may give universal warning:
what saves them is song;
what they *must* do is *listen*.

Dirge for the *Exxon Valdez* Oil Spill

Underneath great waters
swam sea creatures,
clean and strong,
singing songs
later realized as
preludes to cacophony.

Then above them
someone slept who
should have been awake;
a huge floating oil vat
cracked and spilled
a widening shroud.

Otter, gull, salmon,
and sea lion voices
rise on the night wind;
their spirits glide
up to the doors
of village houses.

When no one answers
their calls for entrance,
they slide in silence
through chinks,
down chimneys;
they enter dreams.

"I cry myself to sleep,"
a woman said;
"We are smothered in
death, drowning in
loneliness. Who can
restore the world we love?"

Hanauma Bay Conversation District Closed Tuesdays

On a trip to Oahu, I find a typo in some publicity material:
"Formerly a playground for Hawaiian royalty, the gorgeous
bay is now a Marine Life Conversation [sic] District."

My sister Marilyn
said sea snakes kept her
from snorkeling here,
so I had trepidations . . .

Jacques Cousteau I'm not
when it comes to immersion
in ocean waters teeming
with surprises—some deadly!

But once there, I joined the
crowded ticket line, studied
fish ID posters and warning signs,
readied myself to take a chance.

Then . . . ahhhh . . . submerged
I see a bright gold Threadfin
Butterflyfish and nearly forget
to breathe . . .

Ohhhh, thank you, thank you!
I burble through the tube
as each new fish displays
its watery hospitality.

Oh, Blue Jack! Spotted Trunkfish!
Please send me just one tiny (I've
practiced to say it) Humuhumu-
nukunuku apua'a: *triggerfish*!

Sun-dancing waters resound
with splatterings of hundreds
of talker-stalkers like me.
Afterward I'm glad to learn they're

Closed on Tuesdays.
The whole bay must overflow with
piscatory glee for one quiet day
without Bigfoot Rubberfins prying!

Plagues

On the river boat *Lady Ana*,
   exploring the great tributary
   system of the Amazon,
   some one hundred miles
   northwest of Manaus, Brazil,
   in Rio Negro flooded forests,

we hear stories from
Yarimagua Indians.

In this river, they warn,
as far upstream as
Iquitos, Peru, there are
seven deadly plagues:
      piranha
      electric eels
      stingrays
      caymen (huge alligators)
      anacondas
      candirus (tiny parasitical
         genital-penetrating catfish)
              and
      piraiba (giant child-and-limb-
         eating catfish).

We shudder and feel
less inclined to swim.

Still, our guide says,
in moral terms
we civilized humans—
    plunderers of lumber, parrots,
    monkeys, orchids, fish,
    oil, gold, and silver—
we germ-carriers, slavers,
    and murderers—

we most deserve,
hands down,
the prize for virulence.

Reading Downstream

for Sandra Steingraber, author of
Living Downstream: A Scientist's Personal
Investigation Of Cancer And The Environment

A dictionary spills upstream:
its tangled torrents
of muddied language
flood islands, cave banks.

Words like
mercury, acetone,
toluene, lead,
chlordane, and greed

drown out once common
salmon, crayfish,
mussels, plover,
trout, and integrity.

Stray letters form
misshapen clumps:
DDT, DDE, PCB, PAH,
GenX, PFOA . . .

I screen and scan this
soupy disorder,
anxious to restore
some salutary entries,

Perhaps a few rare
and legible pearls
like potable, pure,
wild, and holy.

A Rat Occasions Reluctant Prayer

Behind the hideabed
I kneel down
in a litter of rat turds.
A urine-soaked mattress
incenses the air.

I confess that
I abhor Sister Rat—
her flagrantly
ill-advised nesting
curdles my core.

I know that You,
gracious God, allow me
to live in Your house—
my human smells
notwithstanding.

Still, I respond to
Her Repugnancy with
poisons, traps, and curses.
If she belongs somewhere,
it's not in my house.

Forgive my impertinence,
but may I suggest that in
Your many mansions
Sister Rat and I would do best
with rooms far apart?

Containment

in the harem of the Pasha of Marrakesh

Flowery designs weave a net
over the concubine's cupboard;
on its narrow shelves
her embroideries,
her kohl, poppy, and perfumes
wait in neat array.

Her tiny cubicle opens
to a sun-dazed courtyard
where tiles echo falling water,
gossip, a peacock's scream.

She glimpses outer gardens
through arabesqued lattice,
bars softened by shadow.

The Pasha calls for her
when it is her turn, or
if she comes to mind,
this woman trimmed to fit
the imperial palace

like the hybrid roses,
pollarded trees, and
carved stucco columns,

like the court musicians
made blind to keep
decadent secrets
from leaking into song.

Ahab's Wife

At first it was enough to keep
a happy child, a warm hearth;
domesticity stitched me
into village ways
while my zealous husband
pursued oceans' mysteries.

Later, my destiny
grew to encompass
more than woman's lot;
my stoic patience ended.
Unmoored from safe Nantucket,
I too fell thrall to the yawning surge.

I became diabolized Ahab and
firm-anchoring wife in one.
My skin smells of lilac and tar,
my mouth tastes of fresh milk and grog;
in sleep I drift between
my white babe and the great white whale.

Rocking my child by the cottage fire,
or straining at oars
with my mates in the chase,
I know whale lines noose my neck.
My mania is not to kill Leviathan
but to fathom its secrets.

Ahab, your savage pride
loosed me on perilous tides.
See our marriage portrait craze
in the rimed mirror of my eyes;
for you, I am now
more siren than bride.

Sedna: A Cautionary Tale

Solar System Object 2003 VB12, one of many
Kuiper Belt objects considered for planethood

Out where a pin-top could hide the sun,
astronomers may have found another planet.
About Pluto's size, Sedna
orbits beyond Neptune.
Remnant of the solar system's birthing,
she's a far-out Ancient One.

Sedna may keep her name only if
proven as a planet, then only if
the International Astronomical Union
finds the name "consistent with
the mythological names of other planets."
Can Inuit override Greek or Roman?

Never mind! Her story's timely.
This Arctic goddess born mortal
grew up so arrogant and vain that
she was married off to an evil man.
Utterly shamed and truly wretched,
she cried "Help!"

Her father kayaked to rescue,
but the husband raised a storm
so bad that her father in terror
threw Sedna overboard.
When she grabbed the boat,
he chopped off fingers, then hands.

He must have been stunned
as her severed parts changed
into seals, fishes, and whales!
Sinking to the underworld,
Sedna became Mistress of Animals
and Goddess of Oceans.

When humans break the laws
Sedna's made for her realm,
she withholds the creatures
they depend on for food.
Then a shaman descends
to make amends for the people.

He combs their misdeeds
from her seaweedy hair.
With abuses like driftnets,
plastic gyres, and dead zones,
we need our own wise ones
to placate the Goddess.

Annie Faces the Atlantic

*On the barrier islands of North Carolina, there are
generations-old stories about horses that swam ashore
from sinking explorers' ships. At Shackleford Banks, off
Beaufort, North Carolina, a guide identified several of these
Outer Banks wild horses, including "Annie," by name.*

Shadowy remembrance
flickers in her blood,
images of vessels in trouble
after long passage to the New World,
disaster narrowly averted by
those horses, her ancestors
who could swim.

Columbus brought mares to breed,
mounts for soldiers and explorers;
Spanish caravels carried some of
Seville's and San Lucar's best
for New Indies' proud use.

Forbears of Annie's "banks ponies"
may have been shoved overboard
in the 1580s from a grounded ship.
They survived by living on
coarse marsh salt grass and
pawed-out freshwater holes.

Annie, a sorrel in sleek summer coat,
daydreams by water's edge;
a sea breeze ruffles her blond mane;
her left hip's branded "25" by
National Park Service caregivers.

Here for a day, carrying food
and drink over by water taxi,
we snap photos and trek through
hot dunes, looking for shade
on this narrow island.

Looming beyond Annie,
a US warship loads for Iraq.
Old and New Worlds mix again,
spawn new histories
of loss and survival.

Madonna and Child Sheltering Supplicants Under Her Cloak

*from a sculpture attributed to Petr Koellin, German,
lindenwood, paint, gold and silver leaf, c. 1470, at the North
Carolina Museum of Art*

Topaz iris petals
flutter fragrance in the breeze;
a bluebird flies to feed
its chicks nearby

while underneath Her gilded cloak
persons whose rank and
privilege allowed them
to savor such beauty daily

are joined with the poor and
lame, saints and martyrs
like this young woman:

Marla Ruzicka,
28-year-old American,
car bomb victim in Baghdad,
who died as senselessly
as the civilians
she served as advocate.

At her funeral mass
the great crowd included,
surely, the hovering host of
dead whose names and numbers
she determined would
not be forgotten.

The stench of
agony and absurdity
rises around us.
Blood stains our hands.
We hear children cry.

Mary, Mother of God,
mercifully bend our
hearts toward the work
of reconciliation, of peace.
Hold Marla and those she loved
forever in Your sheltering care.

I lay a sheaf of iris at Your feet.

Anti-War Rx

Vacation in the
land of your enemies.

Learn enough of
their language
to make small talk.

Listen to their music.

Spend an afternoon
in a park they enjoy;

play a game there
with a child who
looks sad.

Eat a meal
with a family;

visit a place they
consider sacred.

Ask the women what
they love most;

ask the men what
makes them proudest.

Swap stories of
youthful adventures.

Plant a tree there on
"enemy territory" and
see if you can
still call it that.

Designer Earth: A Do-It-Yourself Vision

Meadow in a Bucket; Mountain in a Barrel;
Forest in a Crate; Ocean in a Bottle—
these and other Bio-Paks now
at all Bioregional Branches of
Do-It-Yourself World, Inc.

Meadow in a Bucket
can be color-matched to
your home's landscape palette
(specify perfumed, plain, or allergenic).
Seasonal Sounds Tapes available
(specify Mountain, Seaside, or Urban Park).

Mountain in a Barrel
contains soil microbes and crystals;
these take longer than meadows;
give them to your grandchildren
to teach them patience
(it would help if a volcano erupted nearby).

Forest in a Crate provides
a good intermediate project;
seedlings from Speed-Up Timber
mature in twenty years;
wood mice, deer, and squirrels
available at our Animal Marts
(sorry, some species stocks discontinued).

Ocean in a Bottle recalls
clear water once plentiful.
Placed in our Wave Window
it entertains and relaxes.
Limited saltwater fish still listed.
See Nature Jewelry for remaindered
mother-of-pearl and coral.

Call now! Our Terra Technicians
are available 24/7/365
for custom EcoStyle service.

Night Voice

A bright moon silvered
that warm summer eve.
Leaves flickered in faint
breeze; insects droned.

Daddy stopped the car;
we got out on a dirt road
in a hollow in the hills
near an old sawmill.

"Listen!" he whispered.
We didn't move,
barely breathed
until we heard:

>   whippoor*will* . . .
>   whippoor*will* . . .
>   whippoor*will* . . .
>   whippoor*will* . . .

Over and over

that mystical chant,
like a devotee's mantra,
took us deeper and deeper
into a world of wonder.

Years later, I yearn for
that moment's return.

Poppies

We Americans spoke Spanish
with the young Italian soldiers;
they sang to us as the train sped on;
one of them gave me tender looks
and shyly asked for my address.

Beside the tracks a green
glacier-floured river
slowed to soft and placid blue.
The soldiers got off at a
little station; we waved "Ciao!"

Late June poppies
blazed in ripening grain;
I took photos to remember them
(blurry homages to
Monet, Van Gogh).

Back home I wondered:
why didn't I touch those poppies,
stop to smell them, sit among them?
Why didn't I pick them,
weave them into a crown?

Gorgeous as blood oranges!
I imagined and
never tasted;
Jewels! I thought and
never wore them.

Like a character in a James novel
I'd taken images for reality;
when the tall soldier
sent amorous letters,
I did not reply.

An Urgent Message for Miss Waldron's Red Colobus

First anthropoid extinction in 200 years:
Piliocolobus waldronae, a monkey last sighted in 1978.

High-canopied West African rainforests
once safeguarded your secrets, but British
Museum collector W.P. Lowe's naming you
in 1933 spelled trouble.

He saw nine of you and shot eight,
laid the bounty at Miss F. Waldron's feet.
Neither one of them foresaw
her namesake's shortened lifetime.

Your genus's root word, *colobus*,
a Latin name that means "maimed"
since you lack humanoid thumbs,
was not auspicious.

Your tasty flesh appealed, alas,
to leopards, pythons, eagles, and humans.
Your forehead and thighs flashed bright red.
If only you'd been bitter and grey!

Loggers and poachers despoil your
habitats; your allies have scant funds.
Someone may have heard you calling
in 2006—but since then, nothing—

ominous for a "social and highly vocal
animal." Hunters said you were the
easiest monkey to kill, unable to adapt
to their methods of predation.

Your trust betrayed you.
If you'd only practiced silence
in a once-secure refuge like
Ehy Forest of the Côte d'Ivoire.

Perhaps medicine men can dream
you into another reality. If so, stay there
until—somewhere? sometime?—
a safe home opens again for you on Earth.

Succession of the Gypsy King

*The story is told that whoever touches
the Gypsy King last before he dies
shall succeed him.*

My lord, I am shamed
to have so much magic:
fortune-telling, charms,
divination, and spells,
but none can save you.

If my hands spilled
gold coins and jewels,
I would barter them all
to prolong your life.

Instead, like a mongrel of
dread, love, and greed,
I stand at your bedside
coveting coronation.

Flash—my fingers burn
as your life leaps out!
Frantic for last words or signs,
I jump up, to follow—

Staggered and breathless,
lost in liminality,
I spin wildly between
Earth and deep space.

I hear a blessing as I fall back,
crinkled and crowning,
the newborn king:
"O, my beautiful Romani kin,

May the gods of all outcasts,
the Hermes and Cassandras,
mercifully guide
your wandering way."

Snow Re-writes the World

snow like forgiveness
obliterates
half-truths
the ragged edges
of sly blurrings
smooth into
unsullied
white

on window panes
snow presses
its furry nose
trees retreat
into faint scrawls

tracks on snow:
animal dreams
have feet

snow falling fast
the landscape
more illegible
every hour
lines drawn with
hard grey pencils
replace inky
limbs and trunks

shadows soften to
smudges on
a sad clown's
face

a mime's
barely discernible
white gloves
erase
all worries
in snow's clean
uncluttered world

Opening and Closing Doors: Lessons for Novices

When Thomas Merton asked Thich Nhat Hanh
what he had learned in his first year in the monastery,
he replied, "How to open and close doors quietly."

Test each door you encounter,
its latches and hinges;
look for lurches and lags as
it sways in and out.

Each door is a teacher
as you quietly attend.

Imagine opening or closing
to rising water or to a sunset,
to sirens or to laughter.

Imagine what you'd do if
a beggar crouched there
shriveled with hunger.

Imagine not imagining,
not noticing the door,
your hands, the air.

To open and close quietly?
Neither slam against fear
nor bar the unknown?

Welcome guests you'd
never have invited?

Re-learn each day how
to open to what is?

Opening and closing quietly,
you practice deep intention:
to make a place in the world
for the Buddha and the Christ.

An Unbearable World?

At a climate crisis protest march
I met a man in a polar bear costume;
he posed with me for a photo.

A crowd of polar bear ghosts
drawn by the occasion
brought an Arctic vision
to that muggy D.C. day.

Big as cumulous clouds or
calving chunks of glacier,
they roared outrage
that vibrated the Mall.

These "charismatic
megavertebrates"
star with their cubs
in eco-appeals,
but CO2 still builds.

What will keep their
wild white radiance alive?

In place of an epic or flowery ditty,
I cobble together these SOS lines:
        these bears are our hope;
                they are our beauty.

        These bears are us.

III

Unexpected Allies

Winter Count

Among Plains Indians
the tribal chronicler painted
one summative
annual image on hide.

How shall I depict
this hard time of CLL,
chronic lymphocytic leukemia?

Draw a body pierced with arrows?
a chemo bag, a port?
your tired smile?

Hematopoesis,
a medical term involving
the marrow's blood-making,
evokes poetic license;
I begin a composition
meant as elixir:

Images of roses, those
fragrant royal blooms,
form layers as in
a palimpsest;

From cankered blossoms
now composted,
new leaves sprout
strong and green.

Then, like healthy cells,
vivid blooms of
red and white enfold
you in a healing robe.

Ladybug Quartet

I Ladybug Monday

Bars of Monday's sun
sliced by mini-blinds
cross my disordered desk.
Crows argue against
background traffic.
Spiders web the corners grey.

You, love, drive to the hospital
for weekly blood drawing,
to see if cell counts
spell remission still, or if
your lingering cough
foreshadows malevolence.

Recent visitors shift my focus:
with jaunty helmets atop
black-dotted red flight wings,
ladybugs cruise ceiling moldings,
curtain rods, and lamp shades
though they'd prefer cliff ledges.

These merry invaders,
tireless good luck symbols,
bring a smile, a nudge to notice
the benevolence of small things.
I initiate Operation Airlift and
loft one outside to fly away home.

II Ladybugs on the Ouija Board of My Life

This is weird. I'm reading an article
on the mustard seed parable titled
"The Genius of Small" when *Thunk*!
one of Our Lady Mary's bugs
lands for a closer look.

Another, more secularly inclined,
splacks onto a nearby list of
poetry contests I'm entering.
I say, "Give me odds, Lady Luck,
and make them good!"

Before the mirror at bedtime,
one plinks me a buggy kiss, saying
"It's OK, dear. Pretty is as pretty does.
Me, I'm worried about my kids.
Can you give me a lift home?"

Ladybug planchettes
zap my board with messages
about little things that matter big:
PERSEVERE . . . TAKE RISKS . . .
SAY THANK YOU . . . and FLOSS!

III *Lady Bugg Unbuttoned*

The Lady Bugg is a punster royale.
She loves the Bhugavad-Gita,
any film by Peter Bugdanovich,
any movie starring Humphrey Bugart.

She shops at Bugdorf-Goodman;
Her Ladyship's theme song is
"Bugin the Buguine."

The Lady Bugg waxes ecstatic
when her chef serves peanutbugger
sandwiches with icebug lettuce.

She's a confirmed aphidiziac,
has a peculiar relationship with
a Bunny named Buggs.

Her Bugness' favorite
joke goes like this:
Q. "How do you drive a baby buggy?"
A. "Tickle all six of its cute little feet!"

It's OK to bug her with tons of bad puns
but never say "Bug off!" or "Bugger!"
(not even in whispers—
the walls are bugged).

IV Beetles in Space

Four pioneering ladybugs,
also known as lady birds
and lady beetles,
aboard NASA space shuttle
STS-93 *Columbia* in 1999
won kudos as farmers' friends.

Kids in US and Chilean schools
designed an experiment—
STARS-1 (Space Technology
and Research for Students)—
to see if ladybugs could capture
aphids in zero gravity.

Afloat in their CGBA
(Commercial Generic
Bioprocessing Apparatus),
the bugs, christened John,
Paul, Ringo, and George,
performed famously.

But hey, these are *Lady* Beetles,
co-stars with the first woman
Shuttle Commander,
Colonel Eileen Collins.
I vote to rename them *Joan,*
Polly, Bingo, and *Marge*!

Morning Walk: Searching for Signs

St. Petersburg, Florida

A mallard and a moorhen
guide their chicks around the pond;
a crow teeters and cackles
on the Greenway Drive sign.
In the gutter, playing cards
and two beer cans . . . .

For weeks I've watched
a eucalyptus slough
rough brown bark
from smooth ivory skin.
Its scythe-shaped leaves
splatter the sand below
with pinks, reds, and yellows.

If only human slough,
that grey-gritty dander,
that dusty clogging stuff,
were half so lovely.

On a nearby street, memento mori:
the tail spiral of an opossum
killed nearly two months ago
still oil-stains the asphalt;
crushed teeth and bones in hair mats
(all that scavengers left)
were swept away in Monday's rain.

Back home again, I see
a lizard mate-dancing on our fence,
orange neck-sac pumping,
while wisps of old scales
float out from the new.

Last night I dreamed
I pulled a spaceship out of
a nosedive into a lunar sea,
then piloted it home
to a heroine's welcome.
A clear sign at last?

Perhaps that energetic
lizard has it right:
despite tedium and tatters,
he woos and waits,
trusting prospects of love,
however fleeting.

Jet Lag Fantasy

Like an indecisive amphibian
flip-flopping at low tide,
I'm home to Carolina,
just in from Australia;
I'm ravenous for breakfast
but on Pacific Time.

My lungs mix up
Sydney Harbor ozone with
New Hope Creek breezes;
my thought patterns shift
like a tipsy craft's ballast.

In one ear, soft shuffling
could be noctural marsupials
like quolls, dibblers, or bilbys;
in the other, engines still drone
after hours airborne.

Back among the faithless
mammals who ate our flowers,
who tunneled and trampled
the lawn in our absence,
I think fondly of other
pocketed ones, like the
wombats and quokkas
in Taranga Zoo.

I imagine us all on
US Eastern Standard Time,
swinging in hammocks
on our Piedmont porch.

All the babies and their
mamas snooze the day away
while stowaway koalas,
who've vowed to be polite,
nibble mint from my julep,
a newfound delight.

Kinglet

Warm sun
broke the chill:
in the woods
branches fell,
crackling
free of ice.

Near the creek
in low bushes
a tiny jewel-red-
crested bird
huddled.

When I found
its picture in the
bird book, I read:
Ruby crowned kinglet;
the ruby appears only
when it's alarmed.

Weeks later, I walk
the same path, taking
a break from writing on
a distressing topic—
children and war.

It's cold again,
and I've worn my
red Polartec hat.
Remembering the
kinglet, I chortle:

Here I am,
a kindred spirit—
ruby-topped
but bigger,
seeking respite
from my own alarms.

Love Has No Common Sense

Like the moth who fans
her scent on the night air,
drawing lovers from miles away,
I emitted come-hither pheromones,
and you, principally, came.

Then you gave me the old
olfactory cold shoulder.

I could have been a pint
of spilled brandy,
a loaf of fresh bread,
an acre of rose blooms;
hell, I could have been
a regiment of
skunks in full odor—
you still wouldn't have noticed.

But after a season
of non-amour,
I wafted my fragrance
into the night once more.

Hundreds of silk moths
brought me their finest
cocoons in homage.

These attracted a weaver
who spun the thread,
loomed a quilt,
and totally succumbed
to my perfume.

Moral:
You never know
what No's may lead
at last to a lover's nose
that makes perfect
sense of your scent.

Bluebirds

I'd never seen a bluebird
act so crazy: he swooped
in loops by our garage.
His loud repeated
trilling sounded like
a frantic keening.

For days
I watched the nest box
at lawn's edge,
hoping to see the pair;
but only the male came
and did not stay.

Finally, I peeked in
and found five small
blue eggs, abandoned.
I buried them in the woods.

The next year, another pair
settled in the little house
I'd freshly scrubbed.
I wished them well.

Bluebirds notoriously
keep fledgings secret,
but one morning
a chirping chorus
made me look up
from gardening:

Brilliant blue streaked
the air as parents
urged the babes
out from the nest,
up from falls in the grass,
to trust their wings
and fly away.

Thunder, Fox, and Magpies Speak

at a construction project in Boulder, Colorado

Black-billed Magpie voices
jangle-wrangle from the courtyard.
With obsidian feathers spiking
white-flared breasts and wings,
they swish long sheeny tails
in rhythm with their raucous cries.

What occasions this lusty din?
A Fox! Her dancing black feet pry
for morsels in construction litter
near a Pettibone Earth Mover and
stacks of plywood from Poltach,
Willamette, & Superior Lumber.

Fox's fellow scavengers
love how their jazzy heckling,
echoes in this small live space,
but Western Thunder
drums them into solemn silence,

Rumbles out in righteous anger:
"See these piles of glued wood scraps?
Stolen from our forest homes!
This dirt scraped bare and pounded flat?
The wasted flesh of sacred Earth!
Can't humans ever say *Enough*?"

Then Fox barks out:
"Hey you, Girl, get on down here—
lend the rattle of your tongue . . . "

The Magpies carry on the charge:
"Tell the two-leggeds:
No more stompin' on our feathers,
no more squashin' all our eggs.
Homo *sapiens*—don't we wish!
This nest you're soiling is yours too."

Thus spoke Thunder, Fox, and Magpies.

Spider Woman as Mentor

for Harriet, Tegenaria atrica

She's at peace in my study:
her aesthetic's inbred;
her web equals her needs.

She does not bemoan
an unbalanced diet or
a lack of friends.

She does not say, "If only
I'd learned weaving at a
more prestigious school."

Nor does she complain
she's not a South Seas Spider,
her silk strong as fishnets.

She serenely accepts
her life span of one year
though others have twenty.

Watching her, I whine less;
my own circumstances seem
less sticky, more silken.

Spider Woman-of-Many-Names Weaves Us Into Her Web

As Thought-Woman or
Grandmother Spider,
I name things,
and they appear.
My bodymind labors
birth these lines;
they lead you back
to the Beginning.

As Black and Yellow
Garden Spider
(*Argiope aurantia lucas*),
I am Writing Spider.
I weft words
onto warp I trace
from constellations;
zodiacal mysteries
captivate my prey.

As Arachne or Ariadne,
my sister weavers,
I guide you through
the labyrinth of night;
pitchblack Wolf Hour
yields to dawn
a silver-thread path
cobbled with dew.

Astride the wind,
my web-harp
hums Creation's Song;
I dance a dance
that measures round
your cradle,
your wedding bed,
and your bier.

IV

Mountains and Far Vistas

High-Mindedness

Mount Sentinel, Missoula, Montana

Having a mountain
peering over my shoulder
changes my perspective.
In her light, I review my
complaints du jour:
maybe it's not crucial
that my writing seems stalled,
that my late mid-aged prime
goes largely unnoticed
while my purpose wobbles . . .

Talk about shifting
your point of view!
I compare my six decades with hers:
she's seen mega-change
day after day, year after year,
for over 370 millennia!
When she was part of a tropical reef
she knew personally
such creatures as
little wormlike Pikaia,
ancestor of all vertebrates,
including me.

I'm humbled. I'm impressed.
She counsels that my grumbles
over popularity, productivity,
lost youth and acclaim

could be making (she smiles)
mountains out of molehills.
Why don't I stop muttering
and climb into her lap?

OK. I hike up 1,000 feet
to sit in the grass
while she storytalks.

She points west,
across the valley
to the Bitterroot Mountains,
and tells recent history
she feels I should know:

"Over there Lewis and Clark
risked the Lolo Trail
without guides, through snow
still 8-10 feet deep
in June, 1806.
Some Nez Perce saved them,
leading them safely
through land they knew
as the Backbone of the World.
By the 1890s their friendship
had been betrayed.
Hunted like beasts by white
invaders, their children and
grandchildren fled sacred grounds.

"15,000 years earlier,
their ancestors from Asia
drifted south through these valleys.
They hunted mastodon along
glacial Lake Missoula shores;
its waters would have lapped my feet.
That Lake rocked and rammed
with great ice hunks
until the mountains wept
and broke in cataclysmic floods . . . "

A piercing cry jolts me back
from the long ago—
it's Magpie, flashing black-white-green.
Flamboyant carrion-clearer,
his death-life dance
marks a way to sacred balance.

I climb down
the steep well-worn path,
startled awake—
eyes and ears wide open.

A Sojourner's Views

1

When eleven horses
appear high against the sky,
I remember the horse
I yearned for as a child,
my futile pleas.
Now the mountain and I share
a whole herd!

2

Can the mountain come out to play?
Mount Sentinel trail closed.
Extreme fire danger.
Darn.

3

On an early summer evening flight
from Kalispell to Missoula:
silky blue mountains
scroll west toward China.

4

Feel the wind's pull
on a single feather
your hand holds, swinging;
tremble at the power
of a bird in flight.

5

Tamarack needles on the trail:
fall shed of golden boughs.

6

The sun moves south;
shadows shroud
the creek 'til spring.

7

Mountain Ash berries
bleed through
cottony first snow.

8

We sit in hot springs
with great round rocks—
our faces pink,
theirs green with moss.

9

Tucked in by snowy mountains,
I burrow deep into sleep.

10

The mountain twitches
mule deer ears,
watches to see
what we'll do next.

11

Three grey wolves
braid inky shadows
through willows.

12

Mountain altars
smoke cloudy incense.

13

Runners zip up the zig-zag path
to the University of Montana "M";
I climb those 900 feet too,
but slowly, slowly—
a tortoise among hares.

14

The sign says "Grizzlies sighted here."
We still look for geese at Ninepipe,
but keep a sharp look-out!

15

Mountains to the East
have their privileges—
ours hold back the dawn
half an hour after
it spills through the Hellgate.

16

Mount Sentinel bees
specialize in
Wild tarragon-Golden aster-
Curlycup gumweed honey.

17

My favorite *Missoulian* front page photo:
two male elk, antlers locked in rivalry
over a harem of cows in Yellowstone;
caption: "She's Mine!"

Pont du Gard

for Howard and Rebecca

You skywalk
the top tier
of the aqueduct
once bright with
water for Nîmes.

You trust
your balance
and the skill of
Roman builders
dead 2,000 years.

Acrophobe
that I am,
I cower far below,
head buried
in the guidebook.

"Don't call down
to me!" I'd said,
afraid my fear
would make you
fall.

Sanctuary of the Mountain Sunrise

O Lord my God, you are very great. You are clothed with
honor and majesty, wrapped in light as with a garment.

—Psalm 104:1b-2a

Chipmunks, a wary rabbit
chickadees, Stellar's jays,
Oregon juncos, and
other birds I cannot name—
all scavenge among
piney outcroppings
while the world brightens.

I think of Hopi elders,
of monks, yogis, and mystics
rising daily to witness the dawn.

At my left, in the north,
11,000-foot Mount Meeker,
highest point in this horizon circle,
snags first warming rays;
then they settle, inch by inch,
yard by yard, into this valley.

Like gowns being lowered
over heads and shoulders,
light slips down nearby pines.

Aspens turning gold
cluster in a small ravine;
their burnished tongues
whisper God's words to

Moses at the burning bush:
"Put off your sandals,
for you stand on holy ground."

I peel off socks and shoes,
stand, arms raised high,
on cold rock rough with lichen:

"Holy One, I offer praise this day
for clothing me and all creation
in raiment of your light."

Late Autumn/Early Winter Haiku

cold lake swim
pale sun, yellowing leaves
a loon calls

*

rain beats on tin roof
warm quilt
owl dreams

*

dawn on snowy hills
    a geisha brushes light rouge
        across her cheeks

*

snow clouds thicken
I stir oatmeal
and pack the last bags

*

five black leather gloves
a mismatch of crows
flap rowdy goodbyes

*

empty rooms yawn
clocks wind down
lone cricket claims the hearth

*

back home in flatland
I wonder what the mountains
are doing today?

V

Deep Springs

What Gold Remains

On a day of fog and
rain on bare branches,
the redbud's one last leaf is gone.

That one was gold.
Heart-shaped,
it heartened me.

Like a shy lover's
valentine,
it posted affection;

for a week it fluttered,
timorous and lonely.
I took photos.

Then it disappeared,
its last glide
unseen—to earth

to land among
the beetles and
the mold.

But here is where
I have a choice:
to see this as a sign

of loss and sadness
or of a newness coming
slow and steady

past the darkening,
past winter solstice when
the light increases

inch by inch
as the heart renews
and multiplies in love.

Optics Matter: A Love Poem

When I was eight
I came home with
my first pair of glasses:
I got out of the car,
looked up, and exulted,
"Mommy, I can see the
tops of trees!"

But my nearsighted
habits stay with me:
I notice freckles, lost pennies,
skinks' tails, and ice lace;
I'm a bookworm, a collector
of bugs, stamps, and buttons.

When I'm lost, I search for
lichens on trees' north sides;
I note trail posts or blazes;
but I'm likely to miss
a distant clear sign
like a flare or a beacon.

Which makes me
wonder how we met,
my dear farsighted love,
except that I must have
been focused on the trees,
as usual, while

you saw the whole forest,
still, except for
one moving part:
that was me,
wandering toward you,
and you waited.

Rebecca

with thanks to Leopold Sedar Senghor

Rebecca, your name is like
      pepper and cinnamon;
      it popples like popcorn.
Rebecca, sound of rain on the roof,
      squirrels munching on pine cones;
You, before lightning strikes
      bluewhite energy
      on green fields in deep summer;
Rebecca, sun warmth on cool water
      swimming like a seal, a nymph,
      singing a siren's song;
Rebecca, laughter of the imp
      covered with sugar
      from stolen cookies;
You, girlchild perfumed
      with perspiration and roses;
Rebecca, turquoise star, silver sky lake,
I, your mother, have made myself a sorceress
To name you Princess Maristella of Norns,
Soon-to-be regent of the Sunlit Isles.

Stone Song

You and I are
stones: rounded,
durable, smooth.

Magnets
embedded in our cores
point to each other as North.

In a Japanese garden
we're matched islands
in a raked sand sea.

Thrown into a pool
we make one set
of concentric rings.

We are pilgrims'
dusty tokens
at a roadside cairn.

When our children
are hungry
we make (stone) soup.

Dolmen with
sky as capstone,
we hold druids' secrets.

If Sisyphus rolled *us*
up the hill, he'd double
his luck to go over.

Mary Makes Snow Angels

Mary's graceful body
traces sweeping
alabaster forms;
her laughter evokes
our innocent joy. Oh,
Mother of God at play!

Her angels make us
breathless with hyperbole:
taking the wings of morning,
they fill the sky with the
brilliance of 1,000 cranes
migrating to the moon.

Oceans vie to mirror
Mary's snowy image;
over Arctic glaciers,
every ice crystal
rainbows her presence.

Mary and the Earth
join themselves again
to the Maker's making:
the white ground,
engraved with pleasure,
will melt to feed the
flowering fields of spring.

A Moving Meditation

I'm marooned in a small town
just after Labor Day
waiting for the moving van
already two days late.

Jays squawk and push
at the next door feeder;
the sun blinks on and off
like a shorted lamp
as clouds chug wide
wakes across the sky.

Exposed wires near walls
snake from the basement,
as if hoping to hook up with
something and be useful
(I'm sympathetic).

My fingers feel arthritic
from obsessively cleaning
the 49-crystal chandelier
and seven steam radiator grills
with dust packed like felt.

On penitential knees
I've washed five rooms and
a hall with wood-oil soap,
rendered one lemon and
one Pepto-Bismol pink bath
anti-bacterially pure.

The mailbox is empty.
Only the landlady knows
I'm here; I'm a strange bird
even to the porch sparrows
so chummily chittering.

I boil water for tea
in the one and only pan,
sip and sit in meditation,
resigned to "Zen and bear it."

I make up a koan
for bemused sojourners:
What is the sound of one hand
*   not unpacking?*

Beech Leaves

Beech leaves lighten
the somber palette
of our late winter woods;

like dancers in tawny
silks they line
long horizontal limbs,

follow every
whistling wind
with papery rustling.

Their pale
fragility belies
persisting strength.

Though storms and
time have felled
most other leaves,

they hold fast,
a delicate abiding
presence

until they yield to
winter's slow-
paced dissolution.

When new buds push
this steadfast troupe
aside at last

they exit softly
just as springtime
bursts onstage.

Saint Kevin and the Blackbird

Inspired by Carole Crumley's storytelling
about a sixth-century stone sculpture near
St. Kevin's Cell at Glendalough, Ireland

Holy Kevin knelt in prayer
with arms extended
like cross bars in a hut so tiny
his uplifted hands stuck out

opposing windows. One day
a blackbird took this for welcome,
chose one hand as nest,
and laid an egg.

The faithful saint remained
with arm outstretched;
he cradled the egg until
the chick hatched and fledged.

Who knows whether the
blackbird—the Celts' envoy
of the Holy Spirit—hasn't lit
in your own out-thrust hand?

Perhaps you're entrusted
with a gift just as crucial?
You mustn't drop it or let it
be stolen, chilled, or gobbled.

At night, through storms,
you wonder if you're mad,
but a still small voice
calls you to persevere:

"This egg is a miracle
waiting to be born.
Pray hard for patience;
your hands are God's own."

Tintagel

fabled birthplace of Arthur

In Merlin's cave
Under Tintagel's rock
We stand as pilgrims
In a holy place.

Deep Earth shrives us,
Swallows our misdeeds;
The booming surf
Pours absolution.

A stone-stepped brook
Measures the cliffs
As we clamber
To the summit.

In the North, East,
South, and West,
Coast and sea
Dissolve in mist.

Above and below us
Gulls circle and cry;
They're radiant as doves
In beams of sunlight.

Bright gorse and daisies
Make crowns for our hair;
Among the green grasses
They weave a fine cloth.

A simple picnic
We carried in our pockets
Becomes a feast
At the Table Round.

On the Shore of
Columba's Bay, Iona, Scotland

*As a young monk, Columba—embroiled in disputes which
led to battles killing many men—accepted the penance of
leaving Ireland. He stood here, no longer able to see his
beloved homeland beyond the waves and wept. Legend
says his tears became small green stones.*

I lift my catch of pebbles up,
their cold dark serpentine
still wet and salty from the tide.
Is there a message here for me?

Exiled and repentant for past wrongs,
Columba determined to live as
holy a life as he could wrest
from foreign soil ringed by sea.

With fellow pilgrims, I hike
the green machair dotted with
daisies and spring lambs.
I wonder how he kept faith

when wintry surf—stirred up
by gales no coracle could best—
spread damp chill into hard
beds and scriptorium benches.

In the chapel, wherein
the candles guttered, how
did he bear the howling
that nearly drowned the psalms?

On my own Iona shores,
can I mend nets torn by error
or fate? Will I be able
to survive rough seasons?

I ask the brave saint's blessing
to know such mystery—to
accept bewildered love like his
on my own far island.

machair: *grazing land formed near the*
coast by deposition of sand and shells

Innkeeper's Wife

The stories ignore her
(it's nothing new),
but her strong hands
midwifed the cosmic
glory into human presence.

"Any good birth is a joy,"
she said, "but with this one
my heart felt wildest rapture.

"When he emerged, the earth
reached through my arms
to catch its bliss.

His first breath was a song
the shining angels echoed.
All else was silence."

In depths of bleakest
winter in our souls,
a time of cruel confounding,
we yearn for such a birth.

We search for signs of
love restored between
all women and all men,
between all nations
and all creation.

We trust the Holy Child
waits now within the
womb of life to be reborn,
inviting each of us to join
in hallowèd midwifery.

Praise

We sing a Thomas Tallis anthem
in Iona's St. Oran's Chapel—
our pilgrim pleasure, *a cappella*.

Centuries of chant tuned
these stones in walls as live as a
shower stall and as forgiving.

A dog there by chance with her master
hears "*If Ye Love Me*" in her own tongue
and wags YES! YES! YES!

In a field nearby, elusive birds,
Corn Crakes, rasp a back-up,
their best homage.

I light votive candles
for love, for peace, and for song.
I see them burning still.

www.ingramcontent.com/pod-product-compliance
Lightning Source LLC
Chambersburg PA
CBHW060401090426
42734CB00011B/2216